HELL LIGHT FLESH

HELL LIGHT FLESH

Klara du Plessis

Palimpsest Press
1171 Eastlawn Ave.
Windsor, Ontario. N8S 3J1
www.palimpsestpress.ca

Cover design by Erica Smith
Typeset by Kate Hargreaves (CorusKate Design)
Author photograph by Klara du Plessis
Edited by Jim Johnstone

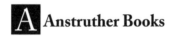 **Anstruther Books**

Palimpsest Press would like to thank the Canada Council for the Arts, and the Ontario Arts Council for their support of our publishing program. We also acknowledge the assistance of the Government of Ontario through the Ontario Book Publishing Tax Credit.

Library and Archives Canada Cataloguing in Publication

Title: Hell light flesh / Klara du Plessis.

Names: Du Plessis, Klara, 1988- author.

Description: Poems.

Identifiers: Canadiana (print) 2020027855X |
Canadiana (ebook) 20200278592 |
ISBN 9781989287521 (softcover) | ISBN 9781989287538 (EPUB) |
ISBN 9781989287545 (Kindle) | ISBN 9781989287552 (PDF)

Classification: LCC PS8607.U17 H45 2020 | DDC C811/.6—dc23

PRINTED AND BOUND IN CANADA

*To Dean, who holds me
so I have room to move.*

Hell-Light Flesh
Turkis Aquamarine
Lavender
Ultramarin-Ultramarine
Softgrün-Emerald Green
Krapplack Rosa-Pink Madder Lake
Rose

HELL

WE ARE AFRAID

That's it. Upstairs,
immediately!
The threat flattens itself against the wall
diminishing in size
by merging with the décor.
Maria's voice adopts a level
frequency, but he is enormous.
I'm trying to diminish my size too,
be a miniature boy child, invisible,
but everything is very real. Now!
I don't want to hear it.

My footsteps cast shadows
climbing.
I can feel his eyes on my back,
uncertain if he's turned away.
It feels like he's staring at me,
but I can't be sure, can't look back.
My back is a slow, vertiginous fall,
dilated pupils, heavy breathing.
Upward mobility means each step away
brings me closer to discipline.
Upstairs is shorthand for
the world is upside down, sometimes
heaven gets bored of having the upper hand,
I screwed up, no fun at all.
The stairs creak far more than usual.
I know now that he's still looking at me.
I know now that I climb so slow
he's turned into the kitchen
a thousand years ago—cooling down,
brooding, the tabletop is an entire landscape.
My back is turned away from my father,
but not in a posture of defiance.
Measure authority in
unfortunate turns of events.
Follow directives exactly, walk
straight, then turn left up the stairs,
touch the banister to illustrate normality,
carry myself upwards, open
armed to hold myself ascending.

I open the door to his studio.
The usual suspects are lined up
around the room—old paintings
pushed to the corners in piles,
not in single file, but stacked and covered,
long-lasting dust accumulates.
Paintings with their backs turned,
deserted, incomplete, or unsold.
Recent work faces forward,
takes a breather, perhaps waiting
for a final stroke of genius.
The word brushstroke includes at once
the quick contact of skirmish
and the immediate violence
of repetition. The strap hangs silently
on a peg beside the door.
On the grand easel, in the good light,
stands the so-called eternal work,
a canvas that'll be done soon, one day,
but also exists persistently.
It's been so patient or maybe impatient,
who knows. I know I've never really liked it.
I've heard him say that disliking
a painting is easier than knowing why
you like it. That's one of the smart
things I've heard him say. Ten to one
my dislike of this painting
is circumstantial. Conditioning.
Unbelievable.
What am I doing here? Teenage chump.
Stuck again among art and behaviour.
If in my small moments

of acquaintance, I'm bored stiff,
he must be so tired of this too—
incessant canvas,
laborious masterwork.

The host of smaller paintings
stare me down. Wow
they really suffer,
snooty stupid kitsch he throws together
to put us through school, I guess.
But stockpile bouquets and bonnets,
namedrop rock formations elsewhere.

His studio is one of the nicest rooms
in the house, spacious layout and all,
would also be my favourite place
under different circumstances.
Perverse that this could be
an immaculate space, no tears,
and so easily done, for example,
if this were mum's studio instead,
not doubling as an authoritarian base.
Amazing how she doesn't really
have a studio at all,
working from the living room,
brushes and palette knives stuck in jars
on windowsills, a ransacking
of table space when guests come over
and cleanliness is called for.
Suppose it's hard finding a house
large enough for five including
Jos, the kid, and me, and two ateliers.
Maria will say, this isn't fun for either of us
so do me a favour, don't make me
send you here again. I won't.
I'll ostracize myself to
the lower floor of obedience.

Wait.

Tread.

Were those steps?

Is he walking towards me

or just round about the house?

What is this, solitary confinement in a house full of art?

An alarm sounds in me,
loud and horrible, engineered
to stir my anxiety.

Listening at the door I can now tell clearly
that no one is climbing the studio stairs.
Who knows how limbs fold,
ambling about or angling up the steps
as they mount. Biology has always been
my least favorite subject. All the nitpicking,
dissection, suction of guts,
and animals in urns like flowers.
There is an obtuse silence
hovering above floor level, breathing
is not quite calm, does not fill the chest
or relax or even let one live.
This is an amphibian silence that camouflages
sound so there's no clue who is moving
or limiting herself to an opinion. Mum?
For once, I have no idea what is going on.
Usually Maria says simply, go upstairs.
So I go upstairs and he follows in five minutes,
but it's been a long time, twenty minutes,
half an hour, I don't know, just the harrowing
sense of time or timelessness.
I really want to get this over with,
but I could also wait up here forever.

Here is a drawer.
The most beautiful assumption
in a studio. That a drawer
is an enclosure for sketches
or the person who sketches.
A three-dimensional space
from which lines line
the imaginative,
the imagist forehead.

The question is the flotation device.
If I open this drawer
and that is the exact instant
that he walks through the door to see
me hunting among his stuff,
would my explanation
be sufficient to ward off
extra anger?
The desperation of monotony,
lasso in confession.
Sure, I regret my willfulness
to the hilt. Still time isn't making
a ripple in my casual lack of concern.
It's an obvious affront.
I need an opening
to stuff thoughts in, to bury
the rugged push of pain
and spare change traits.

When you say feature
an artist feels at ease
even if technically among many
and this is a total group event.

If I keep an eye fixed on the door,
how will I see what's inside the drawer?
Maybe a quick oscillation
between door and drawer,
refusing to get sucked into whatever
contents I might find
and be blindsided
by a sudden entrance.
The negative space of the wooden box
slides towards me, as I glance at the door,
then down. The void
rattles, leading me to the next of a series
of three, all empty. No incriminating
clutter in this table of contents.
Perhaps I was expecting to learn more,
or just divine the tedium.
My father, the upright man,
empty drawers, but well hung.

The dust settling
in the corners of the drawer
speaks to the solitude of recollection.
Red is feral for a boy in need.
Incidentally I
itemize my thoughts
to ground down memories.
My old man is really unattractive right now,
his insensitivity to pain
dunked in among other childhood
malpractice stunts.
But I know where he's coming from—
come on
remember me
in the waiting room of now.

I am savouring my eyelashes slowly.
Lines which run
geometrically parallel,
shadowing the face,
fingerprints or rather
impressionable handprints.
Memory is supposed to be helpful,
but it really isn't
if I know what I mean,
if I know how this feels.
Similarly I blink
so that dust actually enters
my eyes, an excuse
for a tear to sink down along my cheek,
terribly worried that now
I am hardly worthy.

I am waiting,
wasting time
I could be doing something productive
like atone,
tone of voice,
skin tone.

By now I know the handwriting
of my thoughts perfectly.
Plump and too rounded,
but muscular. The kind of writing
that doesn't just grow tall,
but builds strength as it goes,
it ages vibrantly,
writes calves with the understanding
of standing, and presses
physically against its clothes.
I know how this will go.
Maria will clear the table and tell me to bend
over and I'll hold onto the further edge
of the tabletop with my fingertips.
The dust on this ledge is so thick
I can't even write my name in it,
it just clots together when touched.
Dust falls vertically but gathers
into the horizon line of the room.
Run a hand along the tops of everything
collecting dust flatly like a sheet,
then crumple it up collectively.
It resembles writing with a single finger,
perhaps a little finer,
but not much.
The formation of words is integrated
into each segment of each hand.
I'm always impressed when someone
does something with their hand
that isn't the primary hand for writing,
for example, left hand, although
I guess if they're already writing

with their left, right hand is relative.
Loosen every finger separately
before removing the glove.
I consider my footing,
the roomful upturned chairs,
seats on tabletops and legs in the air.

Thought every thought
I could possibly think, I think.
Thoughts knocking about
with the invariable outcome
of inflicting an inner laugh or not.
I draw some conclusions
with the graphite,
charcoal, pastels,
paint, and ink lying around.
The point is to wait,
but the pencil is blunt
and I'm unable to say
exactly what I need to say.

Are you still up there?
(Where else?) Yes sir.
One minute. I called, it's there
and they're keeping it for us.
His voice over the phone is always
a miracle, loud and generous.
I imagine mum falling for him
along the lines of long-distance calls.
He seems less tense, or maybe
I'm relieved. If it's there and undamaged
I caused a lesser mess,
negligence, but not catastrophe.
He puts his arm around my shoulder
and squeezes in reconciliation
that excludes anger but introduces
duty. He says, don't think for a minute
you're off the hook.

HAND

To start again from first principles
and consider the elements
governing the situation.
The hand
holding up its five beautiful digits,
fingers with individual names,
lifelines, the ability to touch,
pick up, and construct.
Mum says her hands are more
elegant when she paints,
the nails elongate,
her fingers slim to represent
images, to hold everything gently.
The hand is also the primary implement
in an over the knee spanking,
the body in prolonged
indiscretion, buttocks hoisted
awkwardly on the lap.
The hand cupped or flat,
cupped to invoke fear but lessen pain
from the sound echoing
in the little hollow of fingers and palm,
flat to hurt with the caveat
of inflicting pain to the hand itself.
When the parent says, this will hurt me
as much as it will hurt you,
he is right—hands sting
their red shadows onto skin.
The hand can also be a proxy.

Take up a shoe, a stick,
a belt, a cane, a spoon,
implements that can then be used
to administer punishment
on a boy whose head is twisted
beneath the disciplinarian's
arm (although this may result
in poor aim). An implement
can also be used to administer
punishment on a boy who bends over
to touch his toes (although it may be
a challenge to keep his legs straight),
or leans over a chair or table
(which may be the most stable
and moderately comfortable position,
considering). When the hand
is extended, the parent
must understand the trick to wielding
their chosen implement—
a belt or leather strap can easily flap
around lacking the necessary dignity
of leather, which needs to be folded
or looped around the hand
to ensure a good hold. Firm aim
and angle are also required.
Lifting and slapping with equally
smooth gestures and rhythm,
pauses between strokes.
The strength of each stroke,
as well as their number,
should be proportionate to the age
of the boy punished

and the gravity of his misdeed.
Fairness and forbearance
are key. The disciplinarian must decide
beforehand how serious the punishment
needs to be—once started
he should not strike out of anger
or lighten his hand in clemency,
but rather stay true to just deserts.
Father and son should discuss the misconduct,
giving the boy a chance to explain
why and how he disobeyed.
It must be crystal clear to both parties
exactly why the punishment is deserved,
delivered to teach a lesson and improve,
but never inflicted out of cruelty.
Likewise, the boy must agree
to stand still, not to flinch, struggle,
or ward off strokes with his hands.
Ritual. Ceremony. The repetition
recognizable in its manner and place
during which judgment is passed.
The boy misbehaved and needs
to be corrected, and it is accepted
that the father gets to make this call.
Ideally, there is a sense of mutual respect,
love, and kinship so that punishment
leads to immediate forgiveness
and renewed clean slate.
Gentlemen's agreement to be inhumane
for a sweet instant.

He slips leather off the wall
and doubles it
double act
double agent
double axe
double back
double bed
double bill
double bind
double bond
double book
double check
double chin
double cream
double cross
double cut
double deal
double decker
double digit
double down
double edged
double effect
double entendre
double exposure
double faced
double feature
double figure
double handed
double headed
double hung
double lock
double meaning

double negative
double park
double quick
double rhyme
double sided
double spaced
double speak
double standard
double stop
double take
double talk
double time
double tree
double up
double U
double vision
double whammy

Over the years, it's always Jos or me, never the kid:

the

se

nse

of

wa

nt

ing

to

c

r

y

but

al

so

not

wa

nt

ing

to,

the

sh

a

me

of

te

ar

ing

thr

ou

gh

the

ge

nd

er

ed

fa

ce,

if

my

sis

ter

c

r

i

e

s

it
is
ok,
her
gi
rl
ho
od
dis
pl
ac
ing
any
bu
rd
en
of
the
e
y
e
s

sa
lt
ed
st
ick
y
wet
we
lt
s
ru
nn
ing
thi
ck
ly
do
wn
ch
eek
s

im   I
ag   am
ine   my
it   own
ne   ha
ver   rd
hap   n
pen   e
s   s
to   s
me,
c
r
y
in
g,
n
o
cl
ea
r
ly

36

/

To feel with emotion
or with a hand.
I feel my disobedience
gather as my whole body becomes
a hand.
To touch as a way to process
being touched.
To mourn with surface.

//

Hand-eye
coordination leaks deep tissue.

///

Through my tears
I understand more clearly—
tinkering membranes—
isn't it strange
that eyes are objects
that one can't see
while seeing through them.
Tears are another
transparent substance
that supposedly blurs vision.
It's a lie. Right now
tears close off nearsightedness
so I can look into my skull,
in reverse,
that's their purpose.

////

One eye always cries shorter
than the other—
shorter in duration,
shorter in the distance
it runs down a cheek,
shorter in the gesture
of wiping away tears
in a single swipe from left to right.

/////

Natural
exclamation
used to express pain.

//////

Ow
Owl
Ow'll
like some new kind of 1st person
accidentally saying, I'll (isle) I will
do better next time
I will do better till the next time I don't do better.
Ow! Ouch!
Okay, recalibrate.
There's a hovering form of emotion
the present a tense question
of the essence.
Syncopate feet
in a momentary eclipse
of posture, posterior
muscles clenched to the uncomfortable limit
when he says,
stand still,
sternly.
I fall back in line.
Countdown is structurally intended
to immobilize,
thoughts kept safely elsewhere,
almost foolproof strategy of absorption
and forlornly wishing it were over,
leaps and bounds of boohoo.

///////

The pain is odd,
punctuated,
flat swathes of time
as damaged dullness,
a physical reminder
of humiliation,
density thickened
or skinned.
So much anticipation
and it's over in an instant,
the know-how to deal with it.

Slack up
so that at once / stroke of luck
suspense breaks down, synchronized,
Maria says, that's it,
conciliatory, genuinely all,
we're done here, let's start over,
but this is my turn and I'm like, that's it!

Welling up, welting, swelled anger,
this exquisite pain
that I bear like an honour.
Physicality, bitten bottom lip
and the remarkable instance that
I am angry now. Eruption of
nervousness no one cares about—
except candy bars—I am angry.
I get downstairs fast.
In my mind I escape out
the side door and into the street,
leaving behind this inconsiderate life.
For real though, revenge fantasies
melt into approximations of saying,
yes sir. Compliance of childhood.
I lock myself in the washroom.
I'm still corrupting my eyes.
Outside on the porch running the length
of two sides of the house and past
my room, the roof's balconied embrace,
Maria enjoys a slow cigarette,
a couple of fingers stuck in a pocket.
Soon he'll rap, two little knocks
on my door, that is,

the room I share with Jos,
which will be a wordless way to suggest
all's good?

Thing is, all is good.
Unsure how it happens, evolution
of emotion, arguably better
to swallow and see to tomorrow
with a smile. Considering
the situation in the semi-
dark, I'm out of options.
Light glimmers without
the certainty of the switch turned on.

In certain circles, you need to
define agency, can't just say,
but have to say exactly
what you mean. Negative
definitions, like not what is,
but what isn't. Opposing clarity.
Here I sit so static,
passivity leaking
into continued sensitivity
and deliberate politeness for a while.
I imagine myself fading
into the reverse side,
pessimistic extremes
interrupting a sliding scale
of slow down
solo.
I am this knowledge alone.
Or rather, I am my knowledge of knowing
alone.

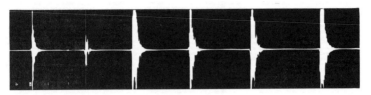

Figure 1: Sound wave starry night

LIGHT

SOUND WAVE

A fissure of pleasure opens,
needling the skin.
The sudden sound
of leather hitting flesh—
contact is the remove eroticism
longs for.

The flinch
exempts not feeling a thing.
The expectation clings
that in the negative space
between where the body was
and where the body reappears
sensation lingers.

(FIGURE 2: WHITE TREE)

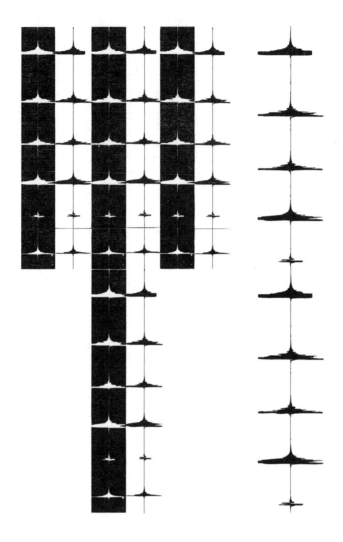

Figure 3: Sound wave forest
Figure 4: Minimalist tree

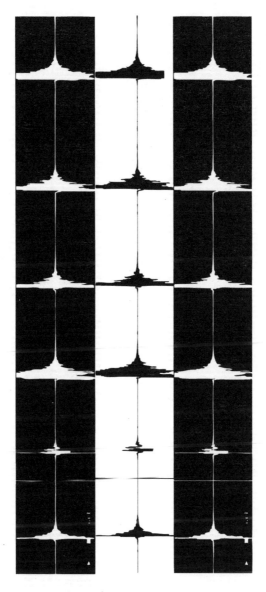

Figure 5: Sound wave trees

The easel is an exercise in self-
sufficiency.
It straddles the space beneath the tree
that is not cool because the leaves
have been lost and replaced
with diaphanous shadow.
Twigs and seeds reflect lines
laced with sunlight
in the dust.

Mum and the kid go into the garden.
Sound waves are a fence
leering behind the ears, pulling the hair
just slightly like an elastic on a tight
ponytail, back to domesticity
where dominance occurs. Mum says,
we are going to have such a grand time,
so the kid sees crystalline palaces,
glacial fairy tales superimposed
upon the yard.
This space, which is the yard,
alternates between front and back.
When it is the front, there are two
moderately sized deciduous trees—
between red and dust,
and before them a vast expanse.
But when it is the back, it is fenced
in and resembles a garden party,
generally green with a lawn
and neighbours who harbour grudges
or are curious. Neither space
seems right for this narrative,
but memory is flippant.
(Remember being scolded for language.
Definitively, the difference between
light and *sky* is a motif.
Pronunciation
a slight hesitation of similarity.
When not articulating the difference,
anger wavers across the face of a parent.
Light translates to illumination,
the quality and condition of shining.

Sky is celestial, heaven if you will.
The difference between
page and *paper* is another motif.
And the grammatical slide
charging from the verb to the noun
for *help*.) Mum and the kid
are avoiding the inside of the house,
or rather mum is imposing
this avoidance, thinking that the sound
of her brother being punished
would distress the kid,
not knowing that she relishes
this sound, or doesn't relish it yet,
doesn't know that she relishes it,
but will come to relish it,
unconscious to conscious shift.

Mum sets up a fold-up easel
for herself, mounting its limbs
into an insect,
wooden from the torso down.
She takes a sheet of paper and clips
it to a thin, solid board
and hands it to the kid
with paint on the table between them.
She intends to use lines as sketches
for sculptures, for lines on paper
to lead to material lines,
solid structures eventually cropping up
in bronze or marble.

But first, collecting the lines,
the outlines of forms, outliers, liars,
lairs of uvula at the back of the throat.
To line a softness, bedding, pink,
comfort in the line, lines
left on the body in discomfort.
Landscape lines. If everything
can be broken down to a dot
and a dot is the smallest particle
of a line, being can be defined
as lines on lines of connection.
Tree lines, leaves, bark, benign
knotted growth of green strength.
Green lines. Green, said to be
between blue and yellow on the colour wheel.
If you include a spot of yellow
on purple, or blue on orange,
or red on green, or the opposite,

it'll pop and your painting will be
a successful navigation of directives.
Yellow always akin to gold,
a kind of softened ochre of veld,
a halo, circular verb
going to the head.
Whereas blue signals the sky.
Tiny entryway
derivative of so many styles and artists,
including the sky in a wall
or any surface which isn't the sky,
including the sky in the sky.
Sunlight, which seems to be
both yellow and blue
as it progresses through the spectrum
to a silence of colour, lays it on hard—
straight lines of transcendental
nature shining down in fists.

Mum suns herself.
Working with the crack
that always seems to run off-centre
down her canvases.

Canvases being new practice
she dismantles them like sculptures.

Boughs round out to the sides
in equal proportions
from a mid-point of symmetry
where reverse eyebrows
sigh up to the divine.
Thin grey branches deign
development, density,
the centrifugal stem,
metaphysical whips
perpetrating crimes to the air—
material scoops of sky
ladled into themselves.

To continue with a hermeneutic
of green, if mum punctures
the canvas along its midriff,
will light or the plastic arts seep
through?

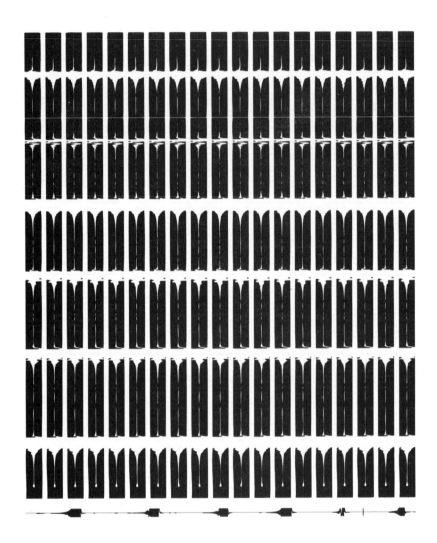

Figure 6: Axis of sound wave fence, or rectangular cross section of light as seen through branches

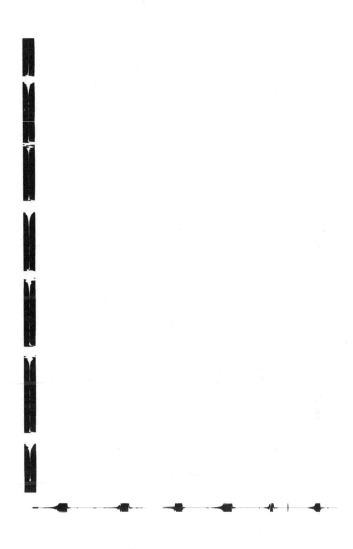

Figure 7: Bamboo fence contusion

The problem with art can be said
to be a gesture that is both
authoritarian and generous.
When the artist
takes matter and builds a fence
around it in the name of the line,
or takes matter into their own hands
and abstracts, what results
is a manifestation of power—
in the sense of imposition
and not in the sense of strength.
Nonplussed by the religiosity
of work, vision interprets blankness
in a way that can be dark,
and what follows reverts to stillness,
displaces creation in lieu of art.
Take the canvas, paper, and clay,
the artist's whimsy boxed up in a form,
transposing headspace onto or into
the medium of composition,
giving that substance no choice
but to absorb this vision,
evolving to belong to its new condition.
Filling the translucent cornea spatially.

Or, the act of proximity to an artwork,
whether from the perspective of the viewer
or the maker, is an activation,
a living force that courses potently
through the eyes and circulates
in the flesh.

The impulse
to author art, equal to the impasse
of staring passively, is rendered articulate
by the massive capacity
to simultaneously imbibe and engender.
Graciously, the eye's posture
doesn't effect sight in the sense that
if one lies on one's side, the line of sight
will still be straight, and if propping
the head up with a hand,
the slant will right itself to vision.
Eyes roll down the face.
To see with sockets.
To see with cheeks.
(Cheeks tease, fixate.
Resist all brutality
in the name of cowardice,
then binge.) Orbs ovulate.
Irises grow and become
gardens. Flowers, with their innate
sensuality filtering like a lens,
encapsulate everything.
To work exclusively with that
which is organic, to pulse through
topics that constantly grow or die,
oscillate voluptuously
while socializing,
moving, stopping, rotating
continually between existing
and not, moderating
the garden party of excellence
in society, conversation, and clarity.

The green edits of grand art
clipping away fineness, finesse.
Uncanny when you look at art
and actually feel something in your eyes.

What if mystically
you were to hurt art?

Here is the rod:

Artist

Parent

Line

Whip

Shading the work with a hand
from the sun. Shading it with colour
so that it expands on the canvas.
Shadow which by definition
reflects its surroundings,
solicits the potential to deflect,
retain and warp the image.
Mum dips her brush into water
so that clarity stagnates, stuttering
elixir of colours mixing and fracturing,
combing the bristles, refining
the surface to mud tones.
Drying her brush with a rag,
she mixes little touches of paint together.
Naples yellow. Sienna. Mars black.
The moment you include white
in paint, you can never remove pastel
from it again.
Eternally diminutive.
Titanium white, its stark glow
of normality, hard grey ore
filed down into a tube.
She lays the colours side by side,
but they spread their gestures,
file away edges, blur the finality
of colour. Intrepid this act
of stirring the palette,
tracing colour combinations,
vestiges of what becomes design.
After a while of responding to surroundings
she stands back, raw umber dawning
on the somber coloration of this canvas,

slow lowering of disdain
for what she has done
or not accomplished this time.
Realizing she's missing foliar green,
blue-green, viridian, teal, forest green.
These trees digressing from liveliness
into livelihood, forgetting their
micro-textured energy, misted rustle,
in favour of failure.
What is this
oasis of dismissal?

(Clearly
reaching hands directly
into the blue pigment of the sky.)

Somedays literally nothing
happens. There is no energy.
No images to gnaw away
at the abdominal clench
of the whole body as earth.
Vivid ache repulsing itself
from production.
Soft suction cup pushing
the self onward, uselessly.

The floss of leaves
switching
back and forth,
a pick-me-up of breathing.

Jos stops by, says hi.
His greeting a mischievous
contraction, a face playing with itself,
his ears expressing laughter. He coils
himself over mum's shoulders
where she sits postured in work.
Jos stands with his legs
wider apart than usual, the light
cast by the reflections through
the window lining him vertically,
an ochre sheen, one hand around
mum's chest, the other hand cradling
his own arm. His face is riddled
by shadows succulents cast,
a viscous mass of slim, aloe-like
branches. They wave abundantly,
ancestors of drought,
but lush in a tended garden,
flame-like contours of green
that surround him.
The thick beige of the living room
curtains bulge in a gust of wind
so temporarily the entire scene
is just a curtain, crisscrossing panes.
The sun moves. The kid's dress billows,
triangular, colourful in the garden.
A voyeur notices poses and roles,
roses, consumerized affection.
Then mum open her arms,
draws her son towards her, holds him, kisses
him on the cheek.
In a slight rustle of cotton and a thigh,
the kid rushes into the rest of the garden.

The yellow flowers are proportional,
grind their big candelabra
arms into the air.
They assemble the base
linguistic impulses of sight,
putting words in the eyes,
eyesight writing—
imagine paint,
the colours' flagship representation.

All the possible art
prescribed by the environment.
Those rock hard yellow berries adorning
the trees' skyline ad infinitum
in itself. Light placenta
shattering the sky in seed.
Primal stamen
petulance.

The elasticity of creating
goes hand-in-hand with violence.
Creasing energy from inside-
outside, managing
the source to bring forth images.
Concatenate the garden,
graft water to greenery to light,
and photosynthesize the ego
till nutrients seep through the face,
and hands and skin leak
in the act of making.
Violence isn't limited to creation,
or the product of creation,
but is wrapped up
in the ability to create at all.
To lay down the law of self.
To flog a rippling which is at once
pain and not pain,
kitsch exquisite,
truly the rich whisk
of finding brutality and keeping it.
To make is a modulation so great
it elongates, warps, contains,
and supplies infinite fodder to fantasize
a newness. Art renews
its plunder and directs its stillness.

This isn't a banal description of pain.
Not the tendency to actually
hurt in a way that confronts and blocks.
Not the oppressive pain
which removes the possibility of all else,
hammers its harmony tritely,
feigns reason in the name
of self-control, brittlely didactic.
No. The soft decadence of feeling
the whole body quiver in tempo,
throbbing reduction
discomfort purgation.
Pain is an eminence, rote original splendour.
(Sorry, prayer becomes erotica.)

In quick succession, the kid
paints many beautiful images.
Her ease mimics the hours
of labour that her parents put in.
She doesn't censor,
she doesn't need to collapse her ego
to get to a place of creation,
pain is still something that dissolves
rather than collecting.
Inflamed emotion first balks then feeds.
Her intention is only to place colour
on paper and this is magnificent
to a point that her drawings
are better and worse than art.
Limerick sensitivity intensifying
a tidy creed into her tiny heart.
She draws, paints a feast
to gift to her mother,
or father or brothers,
sometimes the latter tease her,
but usually she lives in a certain
decadence of acceptance
being the only daughter
and much younger.

The trees announce tiny purple flowers,
fragrant for a while, then
resolved into tight, marble-sized
berries, taut skin slightly sticky,
then wrinkling from green into ochre,
an annoyance to clean up,
dangerous berries

to walk on in bare feet.
The complete perfume of infancy
is wrapped up in the trees'
springtime mauve, moves
to a soft flutter when petals start
to wilt in static relief to earth.
The hopeful window of sunlight
breaks through blossoming
into the nose's catacomb,
microscopic air titillation.
(People tend to see innocence
before they see perversion.)
Rake in the little air throats
open to the world with innocence.

She squats beneath
two trees in front of the house,
immersed in her game.
She is aware.
She builds bridges, scoops
out soil, then lays twigs across
a beauteous tarred highway.
It's hard to keep water in the hollow
though, it keeps seeping away.
Amazing how dams exist,
responsibly collecting vast
quantities of water
for people to drink, to wash,
to include in rituals, sprinkle on plants,
and not only trickle deeper
and deeper into the earth.
The water that just dissolves
into the world must eventually
allow for growth, groaning
as roots tickle and trip up,
drink it in wetly.

Time to go back in, mum says.
She plants her hands on her knees,
a pitiful heaviness
forming at the core of her afternoon.
Denouement contrasting
inside and outside of the home
as oxidizing desire.

Taking apart the easel,
another ritual constant, constantly
making and unmaking motherhood.
Cleaning the paintbrushes properly
beneath the faucet, wrapping tubes
of paint in a linen sheet,
ordering things and ordering the kid
to order her things too.
The finger pressure placed on
tubes of paint, purging,
touch lapping up colour
onto the palette with the faint pleasure of use.
All the heavy tactility consigned to living.
Systems launch their own catharsis,
release friction as peace,
prosaic denial as knowledge.
Her dissidence of distance
maternal fracture
maturely linking in
Maria.

FLESH

COUNCIL OF SOLACE

You think I'm too hard on him,
Maria asks, ambivalence
as agreement by omission,
doubt which should not be felt.
Straighten him out.
He's no longer a boy,
he should know better.

Maria turns left out of the bedroom
and left again into the main corridor,
up the stairs to his studio.
His life has a veneer of confidence,
but the door is ajar and light
filters in from the rest of the home
and also faintly from the street,
though the dark is thick. Paintings
line the walls on all sides, chests wide
open, reaching out from against
the extremities of the room,
bright and welcoming,
contrary to his mood.
Others figure more starkly,
flat cargo exposing worlds.
Maria throws the cigarettes
bulging in his pocket into a flat
ceramic vessel on the table.
The table is an expanse of chaos.
Books with photographs
by contemporaries who'd made it,
so to speak, appearing on shiny pages
with captions and insightful quotes.
A few scribbles in the margins
on a scrap of paper show
the rough silhouette of mum's face,
unfocused in thick pencil,
but accurate, haphazardly drawn
while concentrating on other thoughts.
This slight untidiness of shedding
invites production through solitude.
Emptiness overflows into sediment.

Getting work done is dependent
on boundaries,
taking over receiving time.

He walks over to the large canvas
standing at the back of the studio,
the easel's neck jutting out
and elongating into the air, inches
covered in thick blotches of paint,
accidents of colour straying beyond the frame.
The so-called eternal work straddles
the easel, an enjambment of legs
letting go as it sinks into the cradle
of gravity. Eternity is so precious.
The imperfection of deities
weighing down on the endlessly
long time they have to improve.
This artwork waiting to be complete.
Maria is transfixed, considering options
of betterment, possibly limited
to a brushstroke or two. The pleasure
of oil paint being the ability to add on forever,
enduring work before endorsing,
opening up the rosy hedonism
of the foreground thigh.
That shank that's never been allowed
to channel action, the forward thrust of glute,
that seems to crack out of the canvas,
glut of Latinate muscle streaming
through the body, performing mythology.
What other subject could the artist
ever depend on? Rhetorical,

the traditional expectations of great work.
A visceral hump of mobility
contorted with lust,
lecherous torsion of buttock stepping
toward its own annihilation—
that is what all paintings of inferno show.
The strange lack of trilogy adding
an intermediary to heaven, earth, and hell.
Correctly, Maria takes a step back,
averts his gaze, his protestant context
unforgiving in view of this nymphomaniac
oeuvre of his making,
hurtling out of the hereafter
to stand wantonly in the studio,
bucking and humping at his feet.
Sometimes in moving pictures
the man's backside is so strong that it ascends
while plunging downward on a sofa
in a living room illicitly.

rule
order
command

directive
direction
requirement

guideline
standard

routine
custom
control

practice
praxis
principle

law
statute
mandate

ordinance
pronouncement

dictate
dictum
decree

injunction
regulation

prescription
stipulation

leadership

sovereignty
ascendancy
authority
hegemony

The institution of violence
nullifies critical thinking,
insists on the reign of status quo.
A stability so vast, the cracks
show as weakness, not growth.
Paternalistic restriction is fettered
with emotion—not in the sense
that emotions are a burden,
but in the sense that they lie weighted
down with guilt, humiliation,
apprehension, unrest, self-control,
rote motions of anger, acted
upon undisputed. Each expression
of anger finds the same conduits
of skin to run along,
great, wide expanse of sadistic laminate.

When one can't apologize
due to the logistics of punishment—
I'm sorry I hurt you, it's good for you—
rationalizations no one wants to hear,
rationalizations one clings to
because the intention is benevolent.
When the intention is good
it becomes a system,
when the intention is bad it becomes a sin.
Even though this is not remotely true.

Maiden thinking
seems to lessen intensity
to a hierarchy of age and gender.
Contrast maiden thinking,
as concept, with youth thinking.
Young man on the cusp of adulthood
verdant virility
muscle memory
brain crisp with vitality
cut salad energy
idealism proportionality
restrictive conformity.
Firm hand madonna of morals.

Maria in sartorial machismo,
tailored conduct—
can't whip the baptismal water
and get away with it.

There is a kind of darkness that doesn't exist
because of the absence of light,
but due to its displacement.
That light being cast elsewhere.
Imagine different dark spaces,
cupboards and drawers and nighttime,
the inner body, cavities and orifices,
a great big galactic sphincter.
When the inside's invoked,
there's an immediate darkness.
Obviously a room can be bright,
but only because the outside enters.

The mythological significance
of the past, the father, speaking
through the lip of the present,
unquestioned voiceover.
A soft godliness.
Authority which, in its eternal quality,
lacks contemporaneity, a nowness
that has come undone.
To bequeath tradition onto kindness
is a weird warping, a restructured defiance.
Authority read in gesture, stance, tone,
expectation and stock phraseology.
Rough voice preclusion,
remedy of looking down,
manipulating stature to advantage,
stronger physique, deeper speech.
Being nailed into a trite economy,
expressions of dullness.
Culpability logic mimicking

a lineage of parental antecedents.
Fall back on the mottled light
predefining every word with experience.
Recycling script, gesture, intuition.
Saying what's expected to be said.
This intimidation called love.
Funneling text down the daddy throat,
great big voice box of letters,
divine intervention of the larynx.
Like father like son
and other religious paraphernalia.

Maria sits down
on a functional chair by the table,
his arms draped on
the thin spiraled slats of the back,
unaware that he's stretching
his chest out into the room,
legs spread-eagled into an embrace.
Cathedral says seat like little else.

Stoic, he relegates
his own potential. Silent density
when in a slow reversal of necessity,
in sculptural fluidity,
he contracts.
Legs close in under the chair.
Lap pushes back into an upright posture.
Arms fold in,
then appear on the table in front of him.
Head sinks forward,
dipping into dedication,
this iconographic process of laying
the face on a surface
and breathing in contact,
action melting away to a veneer.
The kind of everyday talk
that keeps things moving,
insinuates politeness. Patina of civility,
a green oxidized sheen
overcoming his body for an instant.
Maria is softening his edges.
Rigid shoulders and perpendicular hips
curve into a bending,

a body burdened with unburdening.
Burgeoning a quick lisp of regret.
He needs to relax more often,
even sitting here without doing
anything real, not working,
parenting, barely being,
there is a tenseness of expectation,
what could be done,
whose will be done,
an unwillingness to take this moment
and say that it is nothing.
Ambition seeps away
into the early nighttime
and the household's deeper breathing,
inhalation redaction.
The plasticity of firmness
vibrates like a muscle.
This studio, this space,
a retention, a coercion,
but also a release, rhythmically
subduing the mind to stillness,
still defined and yet still relevant.

His figure,
lamenting,
uttering,
combing down his children's hair,
the sullenness of this day.
Days which take away
from his ability to get anything done,
being preoccupied with the home's stillness.
The roses on the dresser were a still-life,
have died and should be thrown out,
their beige petals somehow tinged with green.
A quiet so dense it's punctured
by all the daily noises,
but drowsed
to a lissome silence along the spine.

In the room underneath,
accessing her scalp,
mum's fingers dig in deeply,
hair humiliating the surrounding air
with its tendency to expose
bare lines. The hair
that was fastened dissolves,
loosens voluptuously,
and settles as a huge bouquet
in her hands.

GLASS

The absolute strangeness of glass
produced with earth,
the black earth fostering
green shoots and flowers,
a growth of soil.
Sand, silica, mineral quartz,
compounds heated to the silken
combination of a transparent sheet.
This window is a garden.
It passes through me so I can pass through
to the abstracted greens, the blooms,
looming branches that knock up
against the pane, then retreat.
The outtake of reality as framed
by the window, disregarded,
an extraction placed before my eyes.
Windows are ornaments of thought.

Figured glass
decorative emboss
that keeps out prying eyes
screens the shame of hygiene.

The interior soul of a washroom
is always light bluish-green,
a shade of beryl, benign
bandages of touch elongating into a welt.
Anthropomorphic room
that infantilizes me
in a cradle of apology.

The elongated nature
of the washroom,
this cryptic, solitary space.
In the mediated light
of window privacy, quality time
is seeped with a green glow, envy
gentle afternoon pale, sacrosanct
that little latch
on the door sealing me in
from others.

I get that the aim of pain
is to alarm the consciousness
into action. Yet healing insists
on that pain, a reiteration,
continued activation,
restoration treating the skin
to a deepening vector
of tissue's throb and ache.
The warped bruise of glass
puts a finger on introspection
and pushes down.

Green is an old grievance,
tended till malformation
resembles nature. Leafing,
breathing green,
suction can cause a bruise
as much as contact.
This is a representational hurt
guided into territory called healing.

My fingers feel
the sanitized violence
left on my skin and deeper,
in which muscle memory is latent
but inexperienced,
tamely.

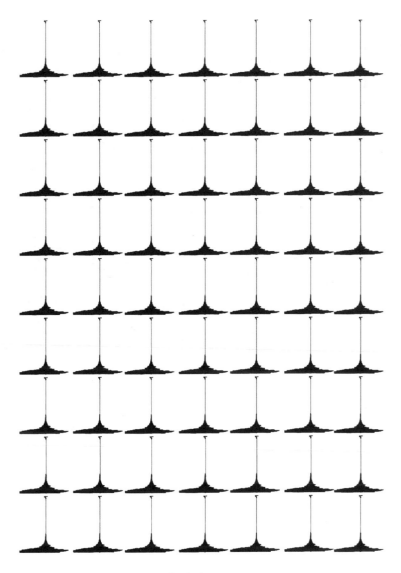

Figure 8: Window privacy daylight

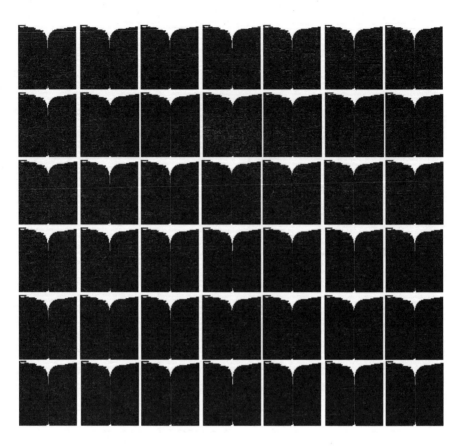

Final figure: Window privacy nighttime

The washroom's foster care status,
I know it holds me.
The tiles, the discrepancy
between those laundered
and the far off smell of used towels.
Soon mum gets
the kid ready for bed.
The kid's fingers smear measures
of a day's activity along her thighs
marking the territory of childhood
on folds hovering over folds,
holding hands with the clap of
fingernails. When the bathroom
door opens, the sound of running
water is distinct and her little voice
something pretty as mum steps
along the corridor
speaking on the subject of pajamas.
Lying in bed under a blanket,
suddenly Jos is concerned,
says, you okay, with the knowledge that I am,
being older, then tells me about his day.
Shut up, I'm sleeping.
Mum walks down the length
of the corridor in slippered feet,
a sentinel of anxiety and rest,
turning down switches
till all light leaks away
and she opens their bedroom door.
Mum and Maria in a universe resolutely.

I walk over to the basin.
In a swift series of actions
I touch the faucet, check
the mirror, contain myself,
fight the downward vector to fling
water in my face.
Drops cling.
The unremarkable crash
of water comforts me,
washes off tearstains.
Then forgets I exist.
After all, water overlooks
originality in favour of dissolve.
The exact same configuration
of water never re-exists. You
can never drink the same water twice,
wash with the same liquid textures,
capture the object of water.
I witness my wet face,
radiant with relief, cautious
to maintain the peace,
resilient in will, collectively
sullen in a way that masks
any real perspective.
My reddened eyes question the limbo
of my age, a young man or a boy.

The pride of living violence.
Its active, living quality,
but also living it,
crossing experience to a sense
of dignity. This hit me
and I am okay. I am strong,
my muscles are lean, I am tall,
I recognize myself, I am beautiful
in the eyes, I am cryptic
in desires that still need articulation,
I am evidence of myself,
I am not denied, I am worthy
of everything, I am okay,
I am physically hurt, I am okay,
I am loved, I am okay,
I am peripheral, but I will be central,
surrounded, less hemmed in,
I am brave, business as usual,
I am beginning to be, or I am
ending and beginning to be on repeat,
I envy age and wait for masculinity
like a prize, a rite of passage,
a publicity stunt, a tentacular
observance, an eyeing,
I situate myself, I resemble myself,
I shake off tenderness
to hum the rocking tune with hard beat
rhythm, I fondle my body,
I am my body, I am hurtled
through violence, I partake
in a tradition of violence, I think
of the violence done to my brother,

I think of the violence done to my friends,
to my best friend, of the violence done
to my cousins, to my classmates,
to the boy next door,
I think of the violence done to my father,
to his father,
I think of the violence
I will do to my son
and it becomes a tenderness,
a passing on, hissing through my teeth,
this patriarchy which is my body,
I feel myself living, I protract
living into thinking, I substitute
living with thinking, I think I live,
I live to think,
I am the only figure of speech
that matters, transubstantiated lean
teenage, I am okay,
I present myself to myself,
I profess intentions, I command
the violence that is a mark, a prize
possession, pride and honour
and participatory, I corroborate
the feedback of my own existence,
the buzz, the noise, the bees sweet
and stinging, I satiate the lingering simper
that rises through monologue to an urge,
an administration of moving forward.

NOTES

All *Figures* throughout are artworks created by Klara du Plessis. They are based on the same internet-generated, found image—the sound wave visualization of the vibrations caused by a belt hitting flesh.

"We Are Afraid" and "Council of Solace" borrow titles from artworks by Thando Mama and Dan Rakgoathe, respectively. These titles are traces from a very early draft of *Hell Light Flesh*, and the poems do not aim to represent the content of the artworks at all.

ACKNOWLEDGEMENTS

Vast gratitude to Jim Johnstone for the delicacy and intelligence of his editorial insight. Thank you to Aimée Parent Dunn and Palimpsest Press for being a pillar of professionalism, and to Erica Smith for designing the perfect front cover. The writing process for this book was extremely private, but there were many discussions with Dean Garlick along the way. This book would have been impossible without the unconditional support of my parents and the months of dedicated writing spent in the Cape Town apartment.

I feel fortunate to be part of a literary culture/community that is both generous and generative. *Ekke* received substantive critical attention, which allowed for relevant quotations on *Hell Light Flesh*'s back cover—words by Domenica Martinello in the *Montreal Review of Books*, by Anna Geisler in *PRISM International*, and by the Pat Lowther Memorial Award jurors, Robert Colman, Brenda Leifso, and Shane Neilson.

A section of "Light" was published in *MuseMedusa* as "Figure 1: Artist In The Garden Evading Violence And Failing," by invitation of Geneviève Robichaud. Two pages of "Hell" were published in *New Poetry* as "An expanse of shivering bright," by invitation of George Murray. A page of "Flesh" was published as a broadside, "Inferno excerpt," by invitation of rob mclennan.

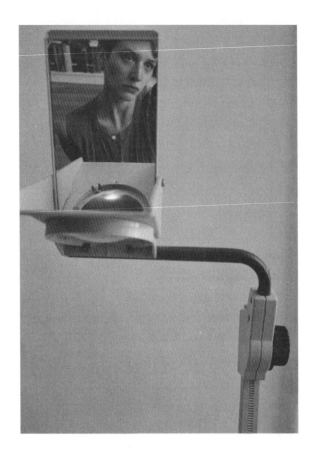

KLARA DU PLESSIS is a poet, critic, and literary curator. Her debut collection of multilingual long poems, *Ekke*, won the 2019 Pat Lowther Memorial Award, was shortlisted for the Gerald Lampert Memorial Award, and garnered much critical acclaim. She lives in Montreal and Cape Town.